CONTENTS

HUMAN

Usain Bolt is the fastest human.
He ran at 37.58 kph in 2009.

What can go faster
than him?

ANIMALS

Animals that hunt must go fast to catch prey.

Cheetah

The cheetah is the fastest animal on land. This big cat can run at 113 kph.

Peregrine Falcon

The fastest bird is called a peregrine falcon.

It dives onto its prey. It can dive at 290 kph.

CARS

Bugatti Veyron Super Sport

This Bugatti is the fastest car you can buy.

It can go at 431 kph.

Spirit of Rett

The fastest petrol car ever made
is called *Spirit of Rett*.

In 2010 it went at 667 kph!

BOAT

Spirit of Australia

The fastest boat is called *Spirit of Australia*. In 1978 it went at 511 kph.

Many people have tried
to make a faster boat.
Nobody has yet.

TRAIN

The JR-Maglev MLX01

This Japanese train is the fastest. It has magnets instead of wheels. The magnets help it go fast.

In 2003 it went at 581 kph!

MOTORBIKE

The TOP 1 ACK Attack

This is the fastest motorbike.
It does not look like a motorbike.

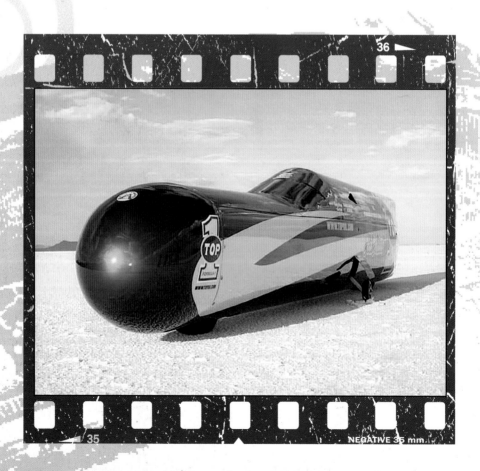

In 2010 it went at 605 kph.

PLANE

The NASA X-43 is the fastest plane.
It flew at 12,144 kph in 2004.

The NASA X-43

It has no pilot. It is launched
by rockets. It lands by
splashing into the sea.

SPACESHIP

New Horizons Spaceship

36

35

This spaceship was launched in 2006. It has no pilot.

The spaceship is flying at 58,536 kph. It is going to Pluto. It should arrive in 2015.

MOVEMENT

The fastest thing we know is light. The Sun is 150 million km from Earth. Light from the Sun reaches Earth in just 8 minutes and 19 seconds.

So light goes at
1,079,251,200 kph.

Now that really IS fast!

INDEX

FOR TEACHERS

About

SLIP STREAM

Slipstream is a series of expertly levelled books designed for pupils who are struggling with reading. Its unique three-strand approach through fiction, graphic fiction and non-fiction gives pupils a rich reading experience that will accelerate their progress and close the reading gap.

At the heart of every Slipstream non-fiction book is exciting information. Easily accessible words and phrases ensure that pupils both decode and comprehend, and the topics really engage older struggling readers.

Whether you're using Slipstream Level 1 for Guided Reading or as an independent read, here are some suggestions:

1. Make each reading session successful. Talk about the text before the pupil starts reading. Introduce any unfamiliar vocabulary.

2. Encourage the pupil to talk about the book using a range of open questions. For example, what is the fastest thing they can think of?

3. Discuss the differences between reading non-fiction, fiction and graphic fiction. What do they prefer?

For guidance, SLIPSTREAM Level 1 – World's Fastest has been approximately measured to:

National Curriculum Level: 2c
Reading Age: 7.0–7.6
Book Band: Turquoise

ATOS: 1.8
Guided Reading Level: H
Lexile® Measure (confirmed): 380L

Slipstream Level photocopiable WORKBOOK
ISBN: 978 1 4451 1609 9
available – download free sample worksheets from:
www.franklinwatts.co.uk